AN ECONOMIC CONSTITUTION
FOR DEMOCRACY

STORRS LECTURES ON JURISPRUDENCE
YALE SCHOOL OF LAW · JANUARY, 1939

THE STORRS LECTURES

PUBLISHED BY THE YALE UNIVERSITY PRESS

An
Economic Constitution for Democracy

By
George Soule

NEW HAVEN
YALE UNIVERSITY PRESS
LONDON · HUMPHREY MILFORD · OXFORD UNIVERSITY PRESS
1939

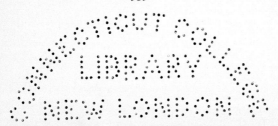

CONTENTS

An Economic Constitution for Democracy

I. THE PERIL TO DEMOCRACY

THERE come moments in the life of the nation when we are surprised by an awareness that the mental season has changed. Imperceptible passage of the days has brought to us new words, new hopes, and new fears; those that lately seemed fresh have withered and fallen, to deepen the soil of history. At such a change of season we need something more than a continuance of the accustomed gradual shift in perception and response. The whole landscape is discovered anew; autumn has become winter, or winter spring; we are obliged to see it all together once more. The old frame of reference is irrelevant and must be made over. If this is not done, we shall be tricked by some assumption, once perhaps true but now without foundation in reality. We shall not know what to expect, or how to adjust our behavior to what is happening.

Such a change occurred when the New Era of prosperity had slid into the great depression—at a date which now can be fixed but then seemed far less definite and dramatic. Another shift of scene came when the depression blossomed into the New Deal. Now we shall awaken any day to the fact that the New Deal itself has vanished and we are again looking at an unfamiliar prospect, the parts of which fit together in a new way. I do not mean by this simply that Mr. Roosevelt's term of office is running out, or that opposition to his program has been increased in Congress. It is not probable that many of the New Deal measures will be repealed or even substantially amended. Nor can it be said that they will pass into forgetfulness without continuing to exert an important influence on our society. What will appear, however, is that they have been assimilated into the background; they are beginning to be taken for granted even by many of their traditional opponents. Our attention is now being demanded by a new situation, which is, to be sure, an outgrowth of the old, but presents a radically different perspective. The New Deal is over; the question now is, what next? To that question it is my purpose to direct our attention in these chapters.

In recent months our eyes have been attracted more and more frequently outside the borders of the United States. First in Asia, then in Europe, we have watched the growth of political and cultural aggressions by militant nationalism, hatreds directed against scapegoat minorities, suppression of liberty, tolerance and scientific humanism, and war itself. As the black shadows have spread across the map of the world, we have read their meaning as a threat to democracy. It is that, but it is more than that. It is an assault upon the whole complex of social ideals that we have cherished, upon the promise for mankind that we have always associated with the birth and destiny of this nation. The hostility that is aroused in us by this movement is not confined to surface interests and judgments; it reaches deep into the irrational sources whence our fundamental loyalties spring. We feel in our bones that here is a menace toward which we cannot but be antagonistic; no propaganda could be so effectual in turning us against it as the propaganda of the facts themselves. It has already become almost trite to observe that the center of attention is now the effort to preserve our form of living against the totalitarian menace.

This antagonism has long been latent in us, but until recently most of us have been content to take it lightly. It was far away; it was not only hateful but also ridiculous and must, we thought, become self-destructive before it became too dangerous. The boasts of the dictators that their systems had a monopoly of vigor and youth, while ours were decadent and must collapse, had sounded like the declamation of melodramatic actors in a bad play. But when Chamberlain strove to reach an accommodation with Hitler at Godesberg, came away with the expressed determination that Britain could not yield to Hitler's threats, and then, accompanied by Daladier, bowed at Munich to the same threats which he had so shortly before resisted, he delivered a shock to our faith in the survival value of democracy.

It was not simply the destruction of democratic Czechoslovakia in itself, or the change in the international strategic situation, that shook us then. And what we felt did not depend on which of the various possible interpretations was placed on the event. Were Chamberlain and Daladier forced to yield because if they had not, Germany would have fought and won? In that case, Hitler's boasts of superior might, which he would not hesitate to use, were those not of a farceur but of a conqueror. Did Chamberlain and Daladier, though confident of winning a war, decline to incur one because they knew a war would bring more disaster than a surrender of the stakes at issue? If that was true, there is no end of concessions to an aggressor determined to achieve world power;

democracy, which must be ruined by war, and has no stomach for it, is doomed in one way or another to give way to a regime that is built for military adventure and thrives on it. Or was Hitler bluffing, and did Chamberlain and Daladier surrender because their nerves were unsteady and their courage weak? Then there is a sluggishness of life and intelligence at least in old-world democracy, which renders it incapable of standing up under strong pressure.

Or finally—and this I believe to be the true explanation—did Chamberlain from the beginning intend to let Hitler have his way, because he cared less for democracy than for building up a counterweight against socialism in Russia, France, and Spain, and perhaps in Italy and Germany as well if they should meet reverses? Then the very fiber of democracy is decayed; its inner integrity is corrupted by the self-same tendencies that are attacking it from without. In so far as we in this country identified ourselves and our values with Britain and France in this crisis—and most of us did so—

our latent hostility toward the totalitarian states became activated by fear. Our self-confidence was roughly shaken; outer menace was reinforced by a treacherous suspicion of inner weakness.

To say that we must be prepared to deal with this danger is easy enough; there is no gain in adding to the warnings and the expressions of indignation at what is going on abroad. But that is only a starting point. We shall have to know far more about the real nature of the threat and develop an effective program to deal with it if our words are to mean anything. It is a matter of course that we ought to be ready to fend off any possible aggression; that is only elementary prudence. But the task is not so simple as this. Britain, France, and Czechoslovakia had been for years more than a military match for Germany and Italy on land and sea and in the air. I suspect that they still were so when the great surrender was made in September, 1938. The essence of the matter does not lie in battleships, tanks, and airplanes, necessary though they are. In order to discover where it lies, we must look inward as well as outward.

The reverberations of Munich will be heard for long to come. We still are unaware of all that it has done to us and to our outlook on the world. The first response was in a primitive direction, as response to raw emotional stimuli almost always is. We, who had for so long been struggling with impersonal and complicated difficulties like unemployment and depression, suddenly were confronted by an external enemy against whom we could canalize our aggression. It is always far easier to use one's energy in hating a foreign devil than in adjusting complex internal realities. And the bitterness of disputes within our national boundaries became for a time subdued as the factions were drawn together by a common fear and a common enmity. We began to talk more of creating a great navy, an armada of airplanes and a much enlarged army; we made preparations to train 20,000 aviators annually in our colleges. The in-group had found an out-group whom it could prepare to punish for its own frustrations and deprivations. And we attempted to include in the in-group all the American nations, which, though many of them are farther from us both in geography and in culture than the peoples of Europe, enjoy the inestimable advantage, in our present scheme of emotional values, of having the same continental home and sharing the same name.

There is a subtle danger in this type of response—the danger that in the process of preparing to cope with our enemy we shall become like him. Defense by imitation is in reality no defense at all. Though we defeat him in overt warfare by growing as sharp teeth, and claws as long and as tough a hide as his, he defeats our detestation of him by impelling us to become a larger version of himself. It is a commonplace that by imitation we grow like those for whom we have strong affection and reverence. But strong disaffection and scorn often constitute the reverse of the same emotional coin and induce their own form of imitation—one which is doubly perilous both because we do not like to recognize it and because it leads to a less happy result.

The theory is not a mere academic abstraction; we can trace its operation precisely and in detail in a situation like the present.

How may we account for the German state of mind? Men and women must suppress a good deal of natural aggression in order to live peaceably in a civilized society. The human animal has at bottom many ferocious traits. But the child is taught that expression of this ferocity brings unpleasant punishments.

Dr. John Dollard of the Institute of Human Relations at Yale, in his recent paper, "Hostility and Fear in Social Life," has well stated a scientific view of this situation. He says, "Since renunciations are invariably imposed on the incoming animal, it develops also hostile attitudes toward these trainers and toward in-group members and symbols; these attitudes include animosity toward parents and siblings and a negative (as well as a positive) feeling tone toward the mores, including religion and authoritarian institutions generally.... The hostility of an animal toward its in-group is a constant threat toward the solidarity of the group and therefore to the continuation of economic coöperation, common defensive operations, and the sharing of a common culture. Such hostility in the individual animal is therefore met with a united hostile front by all other members of the group and is, if necessary, forcibly suppressed. Techniques for accomplishing this suppression range from withdrawal of privilege to a disobedient child to the operations of the criminal law."

As Mr. Dollard further shows, a large part of this repressed aggression becomes, as the psychologists say, "displaced." It cannot be freely directed against members of one's own society, but those who are outside the society can be thought of as inferior, or even as enemies and devils in human form. Against the outsider we concentrate the hostility that we do not dare to feel against members of our own family or tribe.

But this hostility is not too intense, and does not lead to disastrous results, if we can also use a good deal of our aggression within our own group, in socially sanctioned forms. It can find relatively harmless or constructive outlets in a reasonably well ordered society. It is employed in play, in laughter, in useful work, in the competition for power and distinction.

A people that is too much thwarted in these respects piles up explosive emotions. It divides and turns against itself; bitter quarrels grow. The government loses respect and authority. This was for a considerable time the situation in Germany. The nation suffered defeat in war, revolution, burdensome and restrictive peace terms, inflation, and depression. The people were for a long period frustrated by insecurity and lack of opportunity. The government could not seem to do anything effectual either abroad or at home. There were divided counsels, and a rapid increase of mutual hatred and violence between the extreme Left and the extreme Right.

But it is uncomfortable to hate one's own brothers and sisters. Such a society often finds a way to draw off the unused aggression by directing it against those outside the family, who are charged with responsibility for all its ills. Everyone who is in the way is assigned to an outside group. Even if he does not really belong there, a theory is elaborated by which the outside classifications can be made to include him. In Germany their outsiders and scapegoats are called Jews, Communists, and non-Aryans in general, together with foreign states under the influence of these demons. They become the victims. Thus the society gains a comfortable feeling of unity without flaw, of tribal superiority, in which it can adore its own leader and exalt its own tradition. Internal rifts disappear. But since real internal difficulties still exist, there remains the impulse to express aggression against outsiders in wider and wider circles. When one victim falls, another must be attacked.

It is easy enough to recognize this state of mind in Germany, more difficult to discover similar tendencies at home. Fortunately we have not yet become too much like our enemy; but the operation of the same mechanisms may be observed. We also have been struggling with lack of opportunity to work and play, with a general frustration. We had fallen to quarreling bitterly among ourselves. Our rulers were not only extravagantly loved but extravagantly hated. There was a growing prejudice against outsiders—Jews, Communists, foreign immigrants of all kinds. Among certain circles many persons who, because they were in the way or held unpopular opinions, had to be made into outsiders, and were falsely called Jews or Communists. There was a well-established longing to externalize our aggression. At length Hitler was kind enough to provide a focus for these feelings. In the outburst of anger which we enjoyed after Munich, we felt a sudden relief in unity, a sense that after all we belonged to the same family. American traditions were exalted and we prepared to fight the foreigner. But it was significant that at the very moment when we became most angry at the Nazis for their brutalities toward the Jews, there developed an opposition to relaxing the immigration laws for the benefit of the refugees. Anti-Semitism was felt to be actually on the increase in this country. We wanted to punish Hitler much more than we wanted to succor his victims.

From like motives, like actions grow. The German economy has been mobilized about a huge armament program; this absorbs the surplus labor and provides a market for all available material. Productive industry is completely subordinate to it. We hear the same program urged here, both in order to provide weapons against our enemies and to increase production and employment. It is possible to gain adherence for almost unlimited governmental expenditure on defense and to include the needs of our whole economy under this head, whereas it is difficult to obtain political support for adequate governmental spending on relief, housing, conservation, and other enterprises useful in peace. Our shipyards are already busy and will soon become strained beyond capacity; our aircraft factories must be immensely expanded; under the National Defense Act of 1920 a program of industrial mobilization has been prepared and has been explained to industrial managements, which will give many of them enormous orders the moment war breaks out. Then we, too, shall have a totalitarian economy geared to the war machine. These plans have been drawn up with the intention of supplying an army of millions, which would be completely superfluous for protection of ourselves, our possessions, or even the rest of the Americas against invasion but which could be required only for a war on some other continent.

One need not point out to those who can remember 1917 the social and political accom-

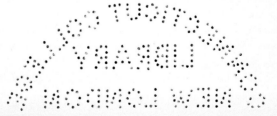

paniments of the war spirit. Its growth means
exaltation of the national tradition without
much critical examination of what that tradition implies. It means a hard and vindictive
national exclusiveness. It requires suppression
of dissident minorities, a moratorium on free
speech and discussion, a diversion of as much
energy as possible from constructive to destructive ends. Much that needs to be done may
be acomplished incidentally in such an effort—
indeed, visitors to Germany or Italy often re-
mark on the extensive road systems, the huge
public buildings, or other showy works of their
regimes—but it also means emphasis on quali-
ties of personality and society that take a terrible
revenge on human beings—on one's enemies
during the process and on one's own society in
the end. In any event it is clear that if we
follow this course because of our anger against
totalitarianism we shall have done as much as
the American character permits to become
totalitarian ourselves.

Let us once more be clear about the necessity

for military defense. To be adequately prepared against a surprise attack is an elementary precaution. We do need a powerful navy and sufficient bases for it, both on our coasts and in adjacent islands in the Atlantic and the Pacific. We need a relatively small and well-equipped army to deal with any expeditionary force that might by some improbable chance escape the navy. It is sensible also resolutely to veto any territorial encroachment by the aggressors on the American continent. But we do not need an armada of thirteen thousand war planes, with the complement of some 150,000 men that would be necessary to operate and serve them, when no potential enemy has bombers capable of crossing the ocean with a military load and returning, or airplane carriers enough to launch more than a few hundred fighting craft against us. We do not need an army of a million or two million soldiers, or the supplies and equipment for such an army. Programs of this kind do not spring from the cool calculations of military experts entrusted with the

duty of preparing plans to defend this nation—
or this continent—from possible attack by the
enemies of democracy. They spring rather
from a subjective need to find an outlet for our
frustrated aggression.

A sensible naval and military program, based
on our real needs for defense, would not in-
volve the expenditure of enough money to end
unemployment or to bring general prosperity.
Battleships of the most expensive type do not
cost more than about $75,000,000 apiece, and
we are not in the process of building more than
four of them a year. Military planes are relatively inexpensive. The reason nations like
Germany and Italy have been able to spring
into economic activity on the back of armament programs is that they have fortified whole
frontiers, trained and equipped great armies
raised by conscription. Nothing less than this
will suffice to carry away the economic peril
even temporarily in a flood of military prepara-
tion. The budget for armament introduced
early in 1939 by President Roosevelt, with its

suggested increase of some $500,000,000, will not add greatly, in percentage terms, to what the government is already spending.

But what is the harm, it may be asked, in having too many planes or too many soldiers? Why not be on the safe side? If we can show any possible opponent a crushing amount of force, he is not so likely to challenge us. And suppose we have to fight our war for democracy on battlefields in Europe, backing up our natural allies who will there be the victims of totalitarian aggression. Then we may need all the aircraft, all the doughboys, all the military equipment we can possibly get together.

The answer is implicit in our former analysis of the nature of the peril. It may become necessary to defend ourselves against enemy states in war—that is true. If, furthermore, the totalitarian regimes come into open combat with the so-called democracies in other continents, there is no doubt whatever that we could in the end make certain that the aggressors would be crushed by throwing our whole weight against them. Rather the doubt concerns the question whether by so doing we can safeguard what we mean by democracy. We were not fortunate in our last victorious war to make the world safe for democracy. Winning wars seems to be a bit irrelevant to the purpose that is nearest our hearts. Negatively speaking, it is essential to defend the democracies against military menace from without. But, positively, it is even more essential to make sure that the democracies are not betrayed by totalitarian forces within. I speak here, not so much of foreign agents or propagandists as of the native states of mind on which these agents work. The reply is, then, that the risk of being absorbed in military preparedness, however desirable weapons may be for practical purposes, is that it will divert us from the fundamental peril. If we let loose our whole energy in hating the foreign enemy and preparing to defeat him on the field of battle, we shall overlook the more subtle but equally real danger of becoming like him ourselves. We shall fail to take the necessary steps at home to preserve and fulfill the democracy we are so eager to fight for. It is easier to be willing to die for a cause than to understand it and to live well for it.

Let us remind ourselves that during the spread of dictatorship of the Fascist type over a good part of the world, not a single nation that has succumbed to it or has even been seriously menaced by it was compelled to change the nature of its society through conquest by foreign warfare. Italy went Fascist as a result of internal forces. By a similar process Germany went Nazi. Japan was not compelled to move in the totalitarian direction by an invading army. Austria surrendered democracy long before the *Anschluss,* and she finally toppled without the striking of a blow. Spanish Fascism originated and grew strong because of the betrayal of constitutional government by Spaniards themselves. Hungary swung into the German orbit of her own accord; Poland, though she is not yet a wholly totalitarian state, has long been ruled by a dictatorship that uses anti-Semitism and opposition to socialism as its chief political bulwark. Even Czechoslovakia, which succumbed to a military threat, was not actually conquered in a fight, and since her betrayal has adopted the totalitarian customs with surprising ease.

When France surrendered at Munich she was being ruled by decree, and almost the first action of her Premier thereafter was to break with the more democratic forces and invite a conflict with labor in both the industrial and the political fields on the pretext that defense against the foreign enemy demanded his action. The British Tories who supported Neville Chamberlain in his policy of so-called appeasement are intensely anti-democratic: his collaboration with Hitler and Mussolini was not prevented by the fact that he came into power on the back of a huge armament program supposed to be directed against the German threat. The ruling powers in both France and Britain have, in spite of apparent considerations of national security, consistently sabotaged the defense of democracy in Spain.

Rumania, though she is now oriented against Germany, has become totalitarian in her internal affairs. The numerous Latin-American dictatorships were not of German or Italian origin. Only a few hundred miles from this city there rules today a virtually Fascist government in the Province of Quebec; yet Quebec has not been conquered by brown shirts or threatened by bombers from Berlin. If all that had been necessary to stop the dictators from exerting influence in the rest of the world had been ability to defeat them in war, they would long ago have been rendered harmless. High explosives and poison gas did not cause the growth of the Fascist regimes and will not suffice to prevent their further extension.

The totalitarian theory and practice is a regression to primitive responses in the face of a difficult and complicated reality. By directing against outside enemies the aggressive drives of a people, it permits these drives to be almost wholly destructive, it withdraws them from the tasks of construction and adjustment and thus produces a satisfying but precarious illusion of internal unity and well-being. Defense against totalitarian enemies merely by hating or fighting them is also a regressive process; it is a concealed imitation of the enemy. Here lies the real peril with which we have to deal. If we do not recognize this peril and act intelligently about it, the totalitarian states can, without firing a shot, bring about the disintegration of modern civilization, just as a criminal act which releases fear and anger can by its contagion make a cruel mob out of an assemblage of good husbands and kind fathers.

The only way to deal with it is to remobilize our psychic and material energies about the tasks of internal creation, thus recalling them from the easy channels of escape into a more primitive mold of life. A well-ordered economy would be a bulwark against what we fear. There are always among us, to be sure, unbalanced individuals who are ready to lead us backward or exploit our emotional or mental weaknesses. But such people are less dangerous when we are busy and unworried, when we have confidence in our society.

The New Deal is past as a period in our history, but even a brief glance about the scene that has superseded it indicates that if the things we cherish are to survive we must struggle again with the same disorders which brought the New Deal forth. The series of measures taken under its name checked the inundations of depression and introduced a number of long overdue reforms. But now that the levees have been raised against the flood, it is time to consider a more permanent and better-articulated program. Emergency remedies are of only temporary effectiveness, and we dare not risk another 1932. As long as one fifth or more of our able-bodied workers are either out of jobs or on public relief, as long as agriculture requires continually increased government subsidies in order to provide even a meager living for most of those on the land, as long as the stream of capital investment on which the future of our whole order depends continues to trickle on an almost dry riverbed, as long as young men and women coming out of colleges and school find few opportunities to earn their livings and seek advancement, there is little cause for reassurance. To submit our democracy to the risks of war or even of a warlike spirit in these circumstances might be an irretrievable error. What must we do to be sound and strong at home? That is the first question we must ask and answer, if we are to be secure against the fatal epidemic which is now raging in the world.

II. THE LEGACY OF THE NEW DEAL

I F the peril now threatening democracy is to be checked, it must be checked primarily by building a sound democratic society. Armament is essential to discourage attack from without, but after all it is secondary to the measures required to prevent disintegration from within. Basic among these measures is an economy that offers to our citizens an opportunity for a busy and fruitful life. In order to discover what we must do to build such an economy, it is well to begin by examining the legacy left us by the New Deal.

Debate about the New Deal on the floor of the national town hall has been loud, heated, and confusing. Most of this debate has been for the purpose of influencing attitudes—to elect or defeat candidates for office, to promote or attack group interests and ambitions. As a result of it, plus what reflection we ourselves could bring to the controversy, most of us have registered our judgments and are eager to pass on to a new subject of discussion. Nevertheless, if we are to know the situation in which we now stand, it may be valuable to look back over the record from another point of view. For the present purpose it is not relevant to assess praise or blame, to justify attitudes wholly favorable or the reverse. What we must do, in as scientific a spirit as we can, is to see the problem of economic security and opportunity for the people of this country as the New Deal has left it to us. In order to be able to pick up the threads at this point, we should go back a little and understand in a more systematic manner what has been done in the past six years.

In doing so let us stand as much as possible outside the recent controversy and forget for the moment the intentions, expressed or assumed, that animated the sponsors of the specific New Deal measures or their opponents. In the interest of scientific clarity it will be useful to view the subject more objectively. Motives are often mixed, and intentions frequently go astray. Let us rather attempt to summarize the more significant activities of the New Deal on the basis of their results—something that now may be done a little better than it could in the confusion of earlier action. And let us relate these results to a few simple and general standards—purposes which, whether the New Dealers actually entertained them or not, furnish admitted criteria for success or failure in safeguarding a democratic and progressive social order.

Let us suppose, therefore, that those put in charge of affairs at the bottom of the great depression had been clearly instructed by the American people to seek the following general ends:

1. *To increase as much and as rapidly as possible the production and consumption of goods and services. This implies, of course, such things as more employment, more*

opportunity, higher real incomes. It also implies the avoidance of downward reactions.

2. *To alter in the direction of greater equality the distribution of the goods and services that are produced.*

Now let us suppose that those who received these instructions had been able, like the general staff of an army, to work out a coördinated and systematic strategy for achieving their objectives. They would have had to proceed on a certain basic assumption, namely, that they could not gain their ends by direct commands to produce more or distribute differently. Ours is an economy characterized by the fact that the amount of production and its distribution is chiefly dependent on money in one way or another. The trouble does not primarily concern physical ability to produce and consume. We have more natural resources, more productive equipment, more technical skill, and more working and managerial staffs than at present we know how to utilize. The amount of money, the rapidity of its circulation, the nature of its division among classes, groups, and individuals, the valuations in monetary terms of goods, services, profits, and capital—these are the major factors with which one has to deal in any attempt to manage the economic process. (I am using the term money here in the inclusive sense of all the instruments that we employ for media of exchange or measurement of values.)

Our strategy board would therefore have been justified in setting up the following four classifications for the kinds of measures it would have to recommend:

1. *Measures having to do with the sources and availability of money.*
2. *Measures having to do with the volume of the flow of money.*
3. *Measures having to do with the valuation of goods and services.*
4. *Any miscellaneous measures not included in the above classifications.*

As a matter of fact, virtually all the New Deal activities do fall within the above categories, and it may be enlightening to discuss them as if they had been so calculated in the first place. A given agency, like the Agricultural Adjustment Administration or the Tennessee Valley Authority, may touch more than one of them, but the classification is useful for purposes of analysis. Let us therefore proceed to assess, according to this scheme, what has been done. While artificial in the sense of description of the teeming detail of reality, it is fairly rigorous as an abstraction of the economic measures.

In a monetary economy, the first necessity for increasing production and employment is naturally to see that there is enough money available. At the depth of the depression, the springs of the money supply were choked. Banks were closed; many persons who owned money were hoarding it. The first action of the new administration was to tackle this difficulty. Confidence in the banks was restored by political action,

including the general closing, the assurance of
the President that none would be opened that
were not sound, the enactment of deposit insurance, and laws introducing reforms into the
banking system itself. Then came a series of
measures designed to increase the total supply
of money. The President was given powers to
take gold out of circulation and to revalue the
dollar, to augment the amount of money by
various other devices, some of which he has
never used. The policy of the Treasury and of
the Federal Reserve authorities was directed
toward increasing bank reserves, reducing interest rates, and otherwise making money available for circulation. These measures were
successful in their immediate objective. Almost
everyone will agree that since the early days of
the New Deal there has never been any shortage, or any danger of a shortage, in the sources
of money supply. The banks have held reserves
far in excess of legal requirements. Interest
rates have been low. The power to issue addi-
tional currency has been almost unlimited.

Devaluation of the dollar, it was supposed by some of its sponsors, would immediately and as if by magic bring about an increase in prices. But the calculus of prices is not solely dependent upon ideas in people's heads—upon what they think or are told things are worth in terms of gold. It depends upon the amount of money people have to spend and upon the supply of goods for which they spend it. Devaluation did have some effect on prices through the change it made in the exchange value of the dollar in relation to foreign currencies. This, however, was relatively slight in its influence and acted slowly. The principal result of the devaluation was to increase actual and potential bank reserves. Not unless this money got into circulation and increased the amount of active purchasing power would its effect be felt.

The policy of enlarging the basic supply of money, though successful in its own sphere, was insufficient to produce the result desired. Though plenty of money was technically available at the source, it was not actually going out

into circulation. Large reserves and low interest rates did not increase very much the total of
commercial loans and deposits, or the issuance
of new capital securities. Consideration of this
matter belongs under the next category. But
before passing on to it, we should mention another source of worry.

It was feared that the greatly enlarged base
for the issuance of money implied a danger for
the future by making possible a disastrous inflation. In the effort to create enough money, we
had perhaps created too much. Those who an-
ticipated immediate trouble of this kind were
mistaken. We have not had inflation or come
anywhere near having it. Inflation is characterized by a rapid rise in commodity prices which
brings exorbitant profits to producers and
traders and injures those with fixed incomes or
salaries or wages. The immediate activating
cause of this rapid rise in prices is a demand for
goods and services which is greater than the
supply. This excess of demand over supply can
occur only when money keeps moving rapidly

into circulation at a time when stocks of goods are low and productive facilities are almost fully occupied. We cannot, therefore, have inflation before we have recovery and prosperity. Money has not moved rapidly into circulation and our productive capacity has been far from strained. It is still possible that, if and when we do approach a new peak of production and full employment, we shall find that we have too much money and that it is flowing into circulation too rapidly. That crisis, however, still seems far away.

We do need to bear in mind the question whether there is a possibility of putting a brake on the circulation of money when the proper time comes without pressing so heavily on the brake that we shall again topple into depression. There is a difference of opinion about this matter among the experts, but at least we have established some techniques for discouraging monetary expansion by Federal Reserve action in increasing reserve requirements, in selling instead of buying government securities, and in raising rediscount rates. Government expenditures and borrowing may also be reduced.

For the time being, then, we can say that the New Deal has left us with at least ample supplies of money.

Next we come to the second category—measures having to do with the flow and distribution of money. The increase in the available supply of money did not in itself lead to sufficient utilization of it. How does this utilization take place? Customarily by private borrowing from the banking system, directly or indirectly. Business concerns borrow money to finance production and trade—to pay wages and buy materials, to extend credit to their customers. Or money is borrowed by them to increase productive facilities. (It used to be supposed that capital issues are bought solely out of savings rather than being financed by an expansion of bank credit, but this is not true in a period of rapid expansion. If money is simply diverted from current consumption or from savings deposits to purchase of capital issues, there can be no enlargement in monetary circulation.) Finally, individual consumers themselves are the recipients of credit.

None of these processes was stimulated to a sufficient degree as a result of the increased supply of money early in the New Deal. Many businessmen did not want to borrow for the purpose of expanding trade or increasing plant and equipment, because they did not have enough advance orders and did not anticipate much increase in sales. Many who did want to borrow discovered that, in spite of the low interest rates, their credit was not considered good. Some who succeeded in borrowing did so not to expand activities but simply to clear old debts and substitute new ones for them.

In the process of stimulating the flow of money the government intervened, as it had also done to increase the supply. It did so by borrowing large amounts—mainly from the banks—and spending the proceeds in various ways. Thus the potential bank credit that was not borrowed and spent by private business and individuals, or could not be used directly by them, was in part channeled into circulation by governmental action.

Three different kinds of intervention were employed in distributing this money. The first consisted of payments to individual consumers, as was done in unemployment relief, the soldiers' bonus, and the compensation to farmers for adjusted production under the AAA. The second was the undertaking of governmental construction projects which involved spending money for both materials and labor, such as roads, public works, housing, TVA construction and the like. The third was facilitation of loans to subordinate governmental units, private businesses, and individuals who could not borrow directly from the banks, as was done through the Reconstruction Finance Corporation, the Home Owners Loan Corporation, and the Farm Credit Administration.

The activities under this category were in part successful, but not so completely effective as those having to do with increasing the supply of money. The ups and downs of business activity since 1933 may be almost exactly paralleled by the increases and decreases of governmental spending of borrowed funds. It is, for instance, a dramatic example of the apparent result of the fiscal policy that the sharp depression of 1937 was accompanied by a complete cessation of deficit spending by the government.

Many people still do not understand that, from the economic point of view, the federal budget was balanced in 1937. The government took in more money in taxes than it paid out to the population—it even retired some outstanding indebtedness. Two changes contributed to this result—first, a diminution in spending; second, collection of a large sum in taxes under the new Social Security Act—much more than was currently distributed to its beneficiaries. What actually happened is concealed by the traditional accounting methods employed, which set up reserves against the collections of social security taxes, increasing apparent government indebtedness as fast as the

collections rose. But these debts the government
owed to itself. It was popularly overlooked that
social-security payments into reserve funds were
merely an artificial bookkeeping transaction.
The depression of 1937 is what we may expect,
under existing conditions, the moment the federal budget is balanced. As soon as the government began to spend out of borrowed funds
again, we began to experience the subsequent
revival.

The spending-borrowing policy, then, was
successful in compensating for part of the lack
of private borrowing and spending. But it has
not been successful as a means of stimulating a
sustained movement of private debt expansion,
capable of continuing when government deficits cease. Pump priming works as long as we
keep priming the pump, but fails as soon as
we stop pouring water in. There is a leak some-
where.

It is possible to identify at least the location
of this leak. The kind of recovery brought by
government spending activates the industries

making and distributing goods intended for the individual consumer—such industries as textiles, clothing, automobiles. To some degree, but not fully, it increases production in the industries making capital goods for use in the construction projects financed by the government. But it has not encouraged a sufficiently large flow of new investment to keep these capital-goods industries going. The mainspring of a capitalist economy—expansion of new productive capacity and long-term investments— seems not to be wound. Therefore private enterprise does not carry on when government enterprise is diminished.

This does not mean that there has been no private capital investment under the New Deal. As a matter of fact we learn from The National Bureau of Economic Research, in its recent bulletin by Dr. Simon Kuznets on "Commodity Flow and Capital Formation in the Recovery of 1932–1937," that revival of private capital formation under the New Deal was substantial when compared with revival of investment in previous periods of recovery. Its absolute amount, however, was smaller than the amount in predepression years. And a large share of the expansion consisted of increase in inventories. Building lagged, as did permanent improvements generally. We need more than we have had in order to keep industry busy and diminish unemployment.

In good years like 1925 and 1928 the net total addition to capital in this country, including public and private building, exceeded $8,000,000,000. The amount did not, before the great depression, fall below $3,500,000,000, even in bad years like 1921. But by 1931 we began to use up more than we created—$4,513,-000,000 more in 1932, $3,506,000,000 in 1933, $2,130,000,000 in 1934. In 1935, revival brought us back to the plus side, but our net capital additions were only $1,517,000,000. In 1936 and 1937 we did better, with $5,524,000,000 and $8,182,000,000, respectively, but 1938 was down again. Of this recent loss, the largest part represents a decrease in inventories.

Why investment lags must remain a matter of conjecture, checked by such facts as are available. The stock argument of conservatives is that private investment is frightened by governmental activities. The stock reply to that argument is that investment was frightened before these activities began, and it was not possible to wait any longer for the fright to disappear. There is much more to be said than is embraced in these controversial generalities. It suffices for the moment to note that here is a crucial difficulty. In respect to its attempt to influence the flow of money, the New Deal has been only partially successful; it has temporarily increased the stream, but the current slows down again the moment it desists from borrowing. Specifically, new investment of private capital in construction keeps on lagging.

GOVERNMENTAL intervention was not confined to providing a sufficient supply of money and helping to distribute it. It is not enough, to maintain a going capitalist order, that money should be available and should be started on its rounds. There may be stoppages in the channels through which the money flows about our economy. If there were not, economic activity probably would not have slowed down in the first place. Or, to speak ethically, some groups may receive too little and others too much. Attention to this aspect of the general problem comes under our third category—measures having to do with the valuation of specific goods and services. For it is prices, profits, and wages that constitute the valves in the system of monetary circulation.

Why is it important to attend to these valves? A few familiar examples will indicate the sort of problem that is here involved. If industries making consumers' goods are depressed or even fail to expand, it is because the consumers cannot buy all they would like to have. A particular industry may suffer, to be sure, because its product is not really wanted, but this cannot be true of all industries at once, as long as the population has unsatisfied wants. And which of us does not? Depression in consumers' goods industries therefore argues either that a great many potential customers do not receive large enough wages, salaries, or income from raising crops (if they are farmers), or that the prices of the goods offered for sale are too high. The problem of increasing sales and production is clearly one of raising incomes of consumers on the one hand or reducing prices on the other, or both.

Another example is the action of the potential investor of capital. Suppose he is considering building a house for rent. He will do so if he finds that the difference between the rent he expects to receive and the expenses of building and owning the house offer him sufficient profit (provided, of course, he can get the necessary loans at all.) But if the cost of building materials and labor, plus finance charges, taxes, and so on, are too high in relation to the probable rental income, he will not build. The problem here is to establish a sufficient margin between costs and prices. In a sense, this example points to the same difficulty as the first. If the rent that can be expected is too low to stimulate construction, that may be because the people who want to rent houses do not have large enough incomes. Or if the costs of building are too high to allow a rent that will attract occupancy, that may be because the prices of building materials, land, and money are too high.

First attention was naturally devoted under this head to those most in need. The really destitute received money directly from the government. But there were many wage earners who had jobs but could not earn enough to maintain a decent living. And there were many farmers who also could not buy, who even were in danger of losing what they had. These classes together comprised millions of persons without whose custom industry and agriculture could not be prosperous. If enough money were to be pumped into the system and maintained in circulation, it looked as if the *rates* at which wage earners and farmers could earn money—that is, the wages and the crop prices—had to be increased.

The New Deal did increase rates of wages, first through the NRA, then by the wage-and-hour law which eventually succeeded it. The same result was indirectly aided through the laws which made it easier for labor to organize and win collective bargaining. The effect of these increases in rates on the purchasing power of the workers as a whole and hence on the activity of industry, agriculture, and trade was severely limited, however, by the fact that employment did not sufficiently increase at the same time. The purchasing power of those who had jobs did grow, but there were still far too many without jobs.

As for the farmers, the attempt to increase crop prices was made indirectly by the limitation of output. Here the problem was complicated by a free competitive market and the existence of unsalable surpluses of important crops like cotton, wheat, and tobacco, which have depended to a considerable extent on foreign demand. Deliberate crop limitation was for a time aided by drought. Then it was hampered by a Supreme Court decision and by good growing weather. Finally it was interrupted in important cases by the natural tendency of farmers themselves to raise as much as possible, especially when prices rise.

The experience of this endeavor leads to certain broad conclusions. Crop limitation, when it can be achieved under the difficult existing social and natural conditions, does raise crop prices. This achieves the intended purpose in the case of commodities like wheat, the demand for which is, as the economists say, relatively inelastic. That is, if the demand does not decrease much with higher prices and increase much with lower prices, crop limitation can bring a larger income to farmers through an elevated price. But in the case of commodities like meat or cotton, which sell in larger quantities when the price is low, crop limitation with resultant higher prices may so diminish the demand as to fail much to affect the growers' total income. In this area the effect on the farmers was similar to the effect of higher wage rates on wage earners whose employment was not sufficiently enlarged.

Attention was also directed to another possible obstruction, in the practices of business enterprise. Neither wage earners nor farmers, in their ordinary state of relatively free competition against thousands or millions of their fellows, exercise much control over the prices they receive or the output they give. Combination or governmental assistance is necessary even to make the attempt. But business enterprise, at least in certain sectors, long ago achieved techniques for doing just this. Actual, overt monopoly exists in a few cases. In far more, the bulk of the production is controlled by a relatively few concerns who normally compete little with one another on a price basis. Prices are fixed in advance for definite periods, and action on prices conforms, with little variation, to the decisions of the leaders. There are "codes of

ethics" or informal understandings, or dozens
of other methods of control.

Business control of prices is most complete
and rigid in certain basic commodities like steel
rails, cement, or glass. It is frequently pointed
out that actual monopolistic practices exist in
but few industries. Do not the automobile com-
panies, for instance, compete with one another? Is there any agreement among them,
express or implied, about prices? It is true that
competition of some kind prevails throughout
a large part of the business structure, but even
here the situation is different from that in agriculture or the labor market. The farmer sows
his wheat, not knowing what price it will
bring. After the wheat is harvested it has to be
sold at market prices entirely beyond the control of the individual grower. The automobile
manufacturer, on the other hand, sets his price
for each model in advance, after a careful cal-
culation of costs. He will make all he can sell
at that price, but the moment demand begins
to fall off, he curtails production. He main-

tains his fixed price at the sacrifice of output; the farmer first produces and then sells the product for whatever it will bring, whether the price covers his costs or not.

The action of the New Deal in relation to the prices and output of industrial goods has been confused and relatively ineffectual. At first the President talked as if all prices ought to rise, and the codes of fair competition under the NRA actually did have the effect of stiffening the prices and restricting the output of many manufactured products. This may have contributed to the failure of production and employment to increase more than they did. Railroad rates have been both lowered and raised. With the passage of time, the opinion has gained ground that industrial prices, and especially the prices of durable capital goods, ought to be lowered. Pressure in this direction has been exercised on steel, on utility rates through TVA and other competition, and on prices generally through the reciprocal trade treaties which have reduced tariffs. A few prosecutions under the antitrust laws have been undertaken. The whole subject is now being investigated by the Temporary Economic Committee.

Methods of taxation are also important in affecting prices and incomes. Here the New Deal has done relatively little by way of innovation. It is an economic truism that taxes on income and profits can be adjusted according to ability to pay and thus can place the burden of governmental expenses on those best able to bear them, while taxes on sales or trade turnover bear more heavily on those least able to pay—a much larger proportion of the population. Arguments for income taxes as opposed to sales taxes rest in the first place on grounds of social justice, but also on the depressing effect of sales taxation on popular purchasing power, which is necessary to create a market for goods. It is contended on the other side that heavy taxes bearing on those with surplus income dry up the sources of investment and discourage enterprise.

Under the New Deal, a larger proportion of

governmental revenue has come from taxes on sales and the like than formerly. This is especially true in states and municipalities. The federal government itself weighted the scales heavily in this direction by the adoption of social-security taxes on wages and pay rolls. The effect has undoubtedly been somewhat to retard sales and employment.

The New Deal has also slightly increased income-tax rates, and has introduced a new tax on undistributed profits of corporations, in order to come nearer to equalizing their tax burden with that of businesses owned by individuals or partnerships. It is doubtful whether these changes have much retarded the investment of new capital, except in the case of small and rapidly growing corporations.

On the whole, confusion still reigns in this sphere of price adjustment. Not only has the action taken been less effectual in accomplishing its purposes than the action under our first two categories, but the theory concerning what specifically ought to be done, even if a way were found for doing it, has been full of contradictions and pitfalls.

For instance, it seemed necessary to elevate crop prices in order to increase the farmers' income. But higher prices for food and cotton are likely to decrease the city consumers' ability to purchase. A price, it is discovered, faces both ways. Likewise it seemed desirable to increase wage rates in order to augment the wage earners' income. But if higher wage rates result in higher prices for industrial products, farmers can buy less of them. Thus, on the one hand, higher prices for farmers do not necessarily mean larger agricultural income if the wage earners' purchasing power for food and textiles is thereby reduced. And higher wage rates, by discouraging farmers' purchases of industrial products, may tend to reduce the volume of employment and thus affect the wage earners' income unfavorably. A moment's reflection, furthermore, discloses that this apparent division of interest between farmers and wage earners is but a crude and artificial expression of a more fundamental contradiction. Wage earners' products are bought, not only by farmers, but by wage earners. Farmers also buy one anothers' products. Is it true, then, that each of us as a consumer, with an interest in low prices, is the enemy of each of us as a producer, with an interest in high prices? If so, an attempt to better the general economic well-being by manipulating prices looks on the surface like an attempt to lift ourselves by our bootstraps.

A similar contradiction appeared in the business attitude toward prices. A natural impulse of a business which is losing money is to widen the margin between costs and profits, and to do so by raising prices of the product on the one hand and reducing or holding as low as possible wages and the prices of material on the other. It is cogently argued that business will not produce except when lured by the bait of profits, and that a satisfactory profit margin is the essential condition not only for the expansion of production and employment but for the enlargement of capacity by new capital investment. But it is often discovered, when this course is followed, that for the ultimate consumers the policy of high selling prices and low outgoing payments means inability to buy. The result is slack sales and the lack of incentive for expansion. Thus any profit in terms of direct costs is eaten up by large overhead expenses due to idle capacity.

What is the clew to this puzzle? Obviously, the New Deal has not found it; the problem of so adjusting prices and incomes that production and consumption may be stimulated is one of its chief legacies to us. We have received, however, a few hints of the direction in which a solution may be found. The first is that, if we are trying to clear the channels for the flow of money which will aid production, it is beside the point to increase all prices by an equal amount. That would leave us in the *status quo*. For everyone's expenses would be increased by the amount of increase in his income. The same logic applies to a universal and equal reduction of prices. The problem is rather one of making internal readjustment among price relationships, of knowing which prices ought to rise, which ought to fall, and which ought to remain unchanged. The second hint is that the adjustment of prices and wage rates is only one factor in achieving the results aimed at. An equally important factor is the volume of production, sales, or employment that may be expected at the prices set. We are really concerned about incomes, and an income equals price or rate or profit multiplied by volume. It is already commonplace to observe that large sales at a low price may bring more profit than small sales at a high one.

Even if no larger profit is earned by low prices and large production than by high prices and small production, the former policy is socially desirable because it enhances the real national income. Large production means more goods and services for the consumer. It means more employment and a greater volume of wage payments. In many cases, if not in all, it is possible to combine lower prices with higher earnings on the part of labor.

To look at the problem from another aspect, we know that as long as there is any unused capacity, material, and labor, and any unsatisfied want, it would be possible for almost everyone to have more goods and services than he now enjoys. But if everyone seeks more income by jacking up his prices and restricting his output, the total result is a more and more severe competitive struggle for a smaller and smaller amount of goods and services. Can the government, acting for all of us, so intervene as to break this deadlock? And if so, how? Under the New Deal, the government has in certain instances intervened in such a way as to appear to make the deadlock tighter—mainly by the NRA price increases and the social-security taxes. In other instances it has taken action that probably relaxed it. But we have had no consistent, well integrated, or effectual policy under category number three.

Finally there is the category of reforms bearing only indirectly on the main purposes. Regulation of the financial markets aims at greater honesty and more publicity, for the protection of investors. This can have relatively little effect on the amount and direction of investment, which still depends fundamentally on the profits made or expected in corporations that might offer capital issues. In the long run, regulation should stimulate greater confidence among small investors. There may be some gain in dampening down purely speculative fluctuations, but such fluctuations are not likely to be removed by this agency. There are measures, such as conservation of soil and other resources, which add to the social wealth of the country aside from the temporary stimulating effect of the money spent on them. The attempt to reorganize the Supreme Court, though defeated in Congress, apparently had its result in the nature of the Court's decisions, which at last opened the pathway for some of the more important legislation under the other heads. Reorganization of the Executive Department for greater efficiency has made some progress. Dozens of minor reforms have been adopted. The new social services, unemployment insurance, old-age assistance, and the like, will to a limited extent broaden the area of economic security, even though the productive mechanism of the country operates at a slow rate. But these things, striking as they are, are peripheral to the central problem. All depend, after all, on the over-all performance of our economy in producing, distributing, and offering employment.

The foregoing findings in regard to this performance, brief and general as they necessarily are, nevertheless indicate rather clearly where the country stands. We have provided enough money and have found many ways to set it in circulation through government spending. These activities have rescued the national income from the depression low but have not sufficed to increase it anywhere near to the level which would be commensurate with our productive capacity. We have been relatively un-successful in starting private enterprise on a steady rise, and especially in stimulating an expansion of new investment sufficient for the growth and health of a capitalist economy. As a consequence there is still a large amount of unemployment.

The most important questions still remain to be answered. How is a progressive and steady expansion of capital equipment to be accom-plished—an expansion which is essential if we are to reduce unemployment to a minimum, use our existing productive capacity, and maxi-mize the national income? What price policies ought to be adopted to clear the economic chan-nels and keep them open? How are these poli-cies to be administered? Finally—and this is a question not raised in the present chapter but of supreme relevance to our general theme—if ways are found to serve these ends, what will be the influence of the necessary new institu-tions on democracy and liberty? Without eco-nomic security and progress, democracy will surely be imperiled. But in the process of obtaining these indispensable conditions, must we sacrifice the very goals for which they are required?

III. THE NEW ECONOMIC CONSTITUTION

THE New Deal has bequeathed to us plenty of money at the source and new methods of channeling it into circulation through government borrowing and spending. Not enough has flowed into circulation, however, to activate our full productive resources and abolish unemployment. Particularly, not enough has gone into new capital investment and expansion of durable goods. Mainly as a consequence of the lack of a sustained expansion of investment, we fall back into depression the moment the government ceases to spend more than it receives in taxes, that is, the moment its economic budget is balanced.

We have also seen that government intervention in adjusting the valves of the economic system through which money flows, that is, wages and prices, has not so cleared the channels as to make possible large and continued production and employment. If it had done so, the pump-priming process would probably have worked in such a way that deficit spending by the government could be ended without a serious collapse of private economic activity. Business would borrow and spend an expanding amount, and a sufficient share of this borrowing would go into new capital investment. This situation sets the framework of our next problem.

Three distinct points of view are now being expressed about the spending policy. The first regards what has been done by the New Deal as a mistake and wants to retreat from it as rapidly as possible. The failure of business to enjoy a sustained revival, and of the flow of new investment to recover, it attributes to governmental intervention itself. The trouble is said to be lack of business confidence, and this lack of confidence is ascribed to a fear of governmental activity, especially to the existence of an

unbalanced budget and a large public debt.
Let the government first stop borrowing, those
who hold this opinion argue, let it cut down
unemployment relief and public works and
subsidies to farmers, and then business will take
up its task and the economic system will right
itself.

The second view is that held by the administration. The borrowing-spending policy is an
emergency measure and will be discontinued
the moment private industry becomes active
enough to absorb the unemployed. But it cannot
be discontinued before then. In the meantime,
we need not be worried by the growing national debt, first because the burden of charges
on the taxpayer is still small in relation to the
normal volume of the national income, and
second because the deficit will automatically
disappear and the debt will cease to grow when
the national income does resume its normal size.
This will not necessitate any marked increase
in tax rates, since higher incomes will naturally
yield much larger tax payments at existing

rates. The administration is unclear, however, about the means of stimulating sufficient revival of trade. It seems to be awaiting a turn of the wheel of fortune in this respect.

The third view is at the opposite extreme from the first. Though held by many, it has been best expressed by seven of the younger Harvard and Tufts economists, in their little book, *An Economic Program for American Democracy*.* According to this view, the idea that government spending out of borrowed funds is merely an emergency measure, to be ended when business revives, must be abandoned. The spending policy should be adopted permanently. Moreover, it should be expanded. The trouble is that government has not been borrowing and spending enough to make up for the whole deficiency of private enterprise in putting money into circulation. The private economy has definitely ceased to expand of its own initiative. Government will be obliged not

* Seven Harvard and Tufts Economists, *"An Economic Program for American Democracy"* (New York, Vanguard Press, 1938).

just to prime the pump, but to operate the pump regularly if unemployment is to be abolished.

An endless enlargement of the public debt does not worry these economists, so long as enough is spent to bring genuine recovery and a continually growing national income. It may be dangerous to keep on enlarging the debt if stable recovery does not come, but if we can borrow and spend enough actually to force steady progress, then the interest charges can easily be met out of the growing tax receipts.

It is unnecessary, according to this view, to try to pay off the debt. Indeed, disaster would come if ever an attempt to do so should be made. People who worry about a national debt that is never reduced, it is explained, forget the difference between an individual's economic position and that of a total national economy. A given individual must of course pay his debts sometime or go bankrupt. But while one person pays his debts, others borrow more. The total debt in the country has had an increasing tendency for years. Whenever it does not increase, we suffer depression. An increase of debt is merely the reverse aspect of an increase of assets. There cannot be an expansion of monetary circulation or a growth of investment without an enlargement of debt. As for the interest burden, interest does not disappear into the sea. When someone pays it out, someone else receives it; internal debts therefore are merely one channel for the circulation of money.

These economists further point out that in 1929 the total debt in the country, public and private, did stop increasing; the growth of the public debt since then has not been sufficient to make up for the shrinkage of the private. Private debt has ceased to expand for a number of reasons more fundamental than temporary depression or lack of confidence. The disappearance of the frontier, the slowing down of population growth, the lack of any great new profitable industry to absorb capital—these have all contributed. What the government must do, therefore, is to take up the task of expansion where private enterprise has left off. It must borrow and spend more and more. In particular, it must channel larger funds into investment in permanent and useful improvements, thus making up for the deficiency in private investment.

What should be said about these three points of view? The first, which calls for a cessation of governmental deficits as a preliminary to revival of business confidence, demands too much confidence on the part of the unemployed, the wage and salary earners who have jobs, the distressed farmers. What assurance is there that business would revive sufficiently, or would not indeed collapse, if government spending and other intervention were withdrawn? Though few people understand the fact, this policy was partially tried in 1937, and with unhappy results. Who knows for certain whether the principal obstacle to recovery is lack of confidence traceable to an unbalanced budget? It seems unlikely. The risk of failure in the recommended experiment is too great. It is a risk involving not merely possible starvation for the unemployed and possible loss of jobs and wage reductions for those now at work but instability for our whole society. No administration, no matter what its theories or its devotion to a balanced budget, is likely to continue very far or very long in this direction before private employment opportunities actually do take the burden off its hands.

In the congressional elections of 1938 there was returned a majority, made up partly of Republicans and partly of conservative Democrats, who opposed the spending policy and had promised to make headway toward a balanced budget. After cutting $150,000,000 from the deficiency appropriation requested for the WPA by the President, they were compelled to restore most of the cut they had made. They then proceeded to vote a much larger subsidy for the farmers than the President had asked. Other appropriations were increased. In the final outcome, the "economy" Congress spent more than the spending President desired. This is not just an accident, or an indication of congressional depravity. It is a proof of the inability of any government to withstand the demand for spending as long as the need for spending exists and it is possible to raise the money.

The policy of the administration is clearly a temporary way of meeting the emergency, but what if the emergency should endure indefinitely? Mr. Roosevelt and his advisers are probably justified in expecting that the customary ups and downs of trade known as the "business cycle" will continue, but it may be optimistic to conclude from this that a time will arrive in the visible future when we shall have such an abundant and stable prosperity as to permit the balancing of the budget and the reduction of the national debt. Short-term fluctuations of business during the past century were but surface movements on a long-term trend of expansion. Have we any reason to be confident that the tide will rise forever? Even the cyclical process itself may be profoundly altered by governmental intervention. In this respect the conservative economists who attack Mr. Roosevelt's policy may be correct. If we are to have a real recovery of private investment, it may be necessary to go through a sharper deflation of capital values, or other price readjustment, than can occur when wages and prices are deliberately shored up. It is true, I believe, that a modern economy will refuse to take the bitter medicine of deflation, but the old kind of automatic recovery may be impossible without it. A policy of waiting for such recovery is therefore dangerous.

The view of the seven Harvard and Tufts economists avoids the misconceptions of the first two. Unless something supervenes like a war or a drastic change in political control that will bring about an economic catastrophe, we shall, I believe, be forced in the direction to which they point as long as private investment fails to revive. Regardless of anyone's theories, there is a world-wide tendency for government to take over economic functions when private enterprise resigns them. Such a basic function as the provision of capital for expansion cannot remain indefinitely unfulfilled. We are coming to understand more and more how important it is. The knowledge that others are not doing this job, and that government can do it, places the theoretical opponents of governmental action in a weak position. Pressures from a hundred directions will in the end overcome their warnings, even though few understand the policy in question or the academic arguments for or against it.

If government is to take over the function of investment which private enterprise has laid down, how ought it to be done? Just spending money on anything may not be capital investment of the sort required. It is correctly pointed out by the authors of the plan that the government has already done much to add to the national wealth by its spending policy and may do much more. A free road built by public authorities is no less serviceable than a toll

road built by private capital. Parks, public
buildings, river improvements, reforestation,
soil conservation—all these things and many
others increase our wealth for the future. In a
sense, investment in them performs the same
economic functions as investment in a new steel
mill or department store. Hiring the labor and
buying the materials creates employment. The
spending of the wages by their recipients aids
recovery. Something of permanent usefulness is
created. Indeed, what is created may be more
necessary and desirable in a social sense than
what might have been done by private capital
under the stimulus of profit. It is better, for
instance, to save fertile soil that could not be
replaced by thousands of years of natural processes than to manufacture patent medicines that
keep people sick. Yet the first cannot be done
under the stimulus of private profit, while the
second often is.

In fact, this logic might be pushed even further than the usual argument carries it. Unemployment relief may feed workers or their

children, who will in the end prove to be a
durable economic asset instead of being left to
become a burden because of the ravages of un-
dernourishment. Or a WPA cultural project
may lead to the production of a painting or a
musical composition which has an incalculable
value for the future in terms of aesthetic ap-
preciation.

There is no lack of things for the government
to do that add to durable values and that cir-
culate income in the present—projects that the
search for profit does not lead private enterprise to undertake. An era of abundance would
require many more of these things than the
New Deal has yet created. Yet the solution for
our difficulties is not so simple as this.

The investment of capital is a basic influence
in determining the direction of productive
effort. Many of the kinds of goods wanted by
the citizens are made by industries now in the
hands of private enterprise. These industries
are not, in many cases, active enough to satisfy
the real or potential need for their products.

The effective demand for the goods in question may not, to be sure, be large enough to stimulate expansion in the equipment to produce them, but that does not indicate any lack of potential sales if prices could be lower or incomes higher. Many people do not eat enough good food or have enough clothing or dwell in decent houses. Though we have a larger number of automobiles per capita than any other nation in the world, there are still many Americans who could use motor cars but do not have them, many who would like better cars than they own. Those who reply, "Why should everybody have a car?" are overlooking the fact that we cannot have full employment in a modern technological society unless consumers are abundantly supplied with things they want. The potential market for electric current is far from saturated. So we could go through the list of commercial products used by individual consumers, finding few that might not be made in much larger quantities. This is an old story. But if that is true, is it not a faulty solution of the problem to direct more and more capital, more and more productive energy, into the projects that government can undertake outside the realm of private enterprise, while we have an insufficient supply of the useful things that private industry does make, and while expansion in these industries lags behind the need? No amount of parks, bridges, and roads will compensate for the lack of enough good food, clothing, and houses.

The same difficulty may be described from the monetary aspect. Both public and private investment may be equally productive in a large social sense. But the consumers do not pay for their enjoyment of a public investment —except enough in taxes to meet the expenses of upkeep and the interest on the debt incurred. The output of a private investment, on the other hand, is bought by the consumers of the product, according to their use of it. It is an important consequence of this difference that public investment does not as a rule tend to increase the *monetary* income of the nation as much as private investment. In our money economy, a large increase in monetary income is necessary if people are to be enabled to buy in sufficient quantities the goods that are offered for sale by private industry—goods that in many instances they want and need as much as the goods that are provided by public projects.

In order to make this point clearer, let us compare a specific public enterprise with a private one of equal cost. Let us say a city builds a park while a corporation sets up a factory, each requiring an investment of $1,000,000. During the construction period, both enterprises pay out an equal amount of money to the community for labor and materials; if the credit for both comes from banks, the national income is increased by a like amount in each case during the construction period. But after the projects are finished, the park is opened free to one and all; the city continues to employ only the staff necessary for maintenance, collecting out of taxes the money to remunerate

the working force and pay the interest. Let us
say this costs $50,000 annually. But the factory,
if it is successful, sells its products and does a
business of, say $500,000 a year. Out of this it
pays for wages, materials, profits, and interest.
It is clear that the existence of the factory, after
it is finished, adds more to the national money
income than does the existence of the park,
provided the money to keep the factory going
is available.

The difference does not lie solely in the
difference of the physical nature of the two enterprises. If the park were a private enterprise,
and admission were charged to it, more money
would be kept in circulation than under the
city's custom of permitting free use. The park
does not, after it is built, keep money in circulation to as great an extent in proportion to
the investment as does the factory. A much
larger amount of public investment than of
private is therefore required to build up a national income of a given size. The usual type
of public investment is not, over a period of

time, so efficient in providing the circulation of money required to pay for the goods that people have to buy.

Of course there is no intrinsic benefit in a large money income, provided that equivalent real values may be obtained for a small one. We might conceivably have an immense national product without any monetary income at all if the government should enter every form of production, giving away the output, and paying no wages—provided we assume that people would do the work purely out of a sense of obligation for the goods they received. But an indefinitely expanding program of public investment in producing so-called free goods, carried out in the midst of an economic order which leaves a large part of its work to private enterprise, is likely to create distortion in our schedules of production and consumption.

These considerations lead us to the conclusion that if governmental intervention is to be relied upon to restore that upward trend of capital investment which is necessary, it must do something about fields now occupied by private enterprise as well as about the projects which are noncommercial in nature. Somehow or other, there must be a much larger expansion in the production of goods and services ordinarily sold to the consumers, as well as of goods and services customarily paid for only by taxation.

But here we encounter the opinion of our seven economists that the opportunity for expansion of private enterprise has been lost by the disappearance of the frontier, the slowing down in population growth, and other like circumstances. It is true that for nearly ten years there has been little increase in the total of private investment—indeed, in some of these years there has been a net loss in the amount already in existence. Possibly the obstacles are too great for private enterprise to overcome, at least for a long time. But I believe the main obstacles lie in a different direction from those cited and are not insuperable. As long as many people want more of the goods that industry makes, there is no fundamental reason why it cannot expand. Our productive equipment now is nowhere near sufficient to turn out the goods that the population would undoubtedly buy if the purchasing power of the average family were raised even to a moderate level. We do not need new physical frontiers or a large growth of population or even new industries if we will set ourselves to the task of supplying the wants already existing. The problem is therefore one of increasing money incomes or reducing prices, or both. We are back at the point where we found the New Deal had been least successful, that is, in adjusting the valves of the economic system so that money would keep on flowing, once it had been spent from a primary source.

It is worth taking a moment here to consider one frequent objection to the proposition that an opportunity exists for more employment through industrial expansion. Rapid improvement of technology, it is said, makes it possible to enlarge industrial production without paying out more in wages and even without great investment in new plant. That is true. But in so far as it is true, it results in reduced unit cost of production and hence makes possible still further reduction of prices. If this course is followed, it ought to lead to a compensating enlargement of sales, so long as the real want for the product is not satisfied. The time could come when larger productive equipment would be needed. The basic problem still remains one of the relationship of prices and incomes.

If we look at the figures, we actually do find a considerable increase of new capital investment in manufacturing industry during recent periods of revival, just as we have found temporary rapid enlargement in the markets for consumers' goods. The sticking point of recovery has apparently not been in manufacturing for the individual consumer. The reason that heavy industries making durable or capital goods have suffered setbacks, have thrown workers out of employment, and have thus dampened down the industries making con-

sumers' goods, is that the customary basic outlets upon which the heavy industries have
relied in the past have not resumed their expansion. The three great channels for new investment in the years before 1929 had been:
first, building construction; second, railroads;
third, public utilities. And the deficiency in
new investment has occurred since 1929 mainly
in these three industries. If they were active
and expanding, their payments for labor and
orders for materials would keep the heavy
manufacturing industries busy, and we could
resume the long-term upward trend.

In not one of these old stand-bys of investment is there any lack of real want for the
product. Need for better and less-crowded
housing is almost unlimited, especially on the
part of the half of our population in the lower
income brackets. Saturation points in the use
of electricity or even of gas are still far in the
future. Railroads have met severe competition
recently, it is true, and the era of adding mile-
age is probably at an end, yet there is a great

need for new equipment and more mainte-
nance. And it has been demonstrated that better
service and lower rates would attract much
more business to the railways.

In each of these fields governmental intervention may clear the channels for new investment
if it will adjust properly the cost and price
factors. Private building is tied up in a tangle
of frozen debts, high prices for materials, and
medieval inefficiency. Yet experience both
here and abroad has demonstrated that large-
scale housing projects, properly planned and
financed, can offer such a good product at such
low rentals that investment in housing which
looks only for a moderate return is one of the
safest in the world. The opportunity here is
immense if technical and legal obstacles and
political opposition can be overcome. Public
utilities need only a straightening out of their
financial structures and sufficiently low rates in
order to tap an indefinitely larger market. The
railroad problem is complicated, but its essen-
tials are clear. Writing down of burdensome

capital structures, better service, economy through unified operation, and lower rates will certainly help.

Government would be ill-advised to pour capital into any of these fields so long as they are hampered by the existing difficulties of private enterprise, which inhibit their possibilities of growth. But in each of them, government enterprise has the opportunity to enter in such a manner that these inhibitions can be removed, and the way opened for useful new investment. It has already begun to do so in housing and utilities; I believe it will be compelled to do so in railroads also. The great advantage in the turning of government enterprise to investment channels like this, which have become clogged under private enterprise, is that freeing them will contribute immensely to the expansion of monetary income in the nation to an extent that government enterprise ordinarily has not.

Meanwhile, the government should continue to study price problems in general, so that, even in the fields which it is not compelled to administer, necessary corrections may be made. In some cases publicity and the discovery of guiding principles may be enough. In others it may be necessary—and possible—to enforce competition. In still others regulation of new types may be employed. The ultimate recourse, if other methods fail, would always be reorganization as a public enterprise. All this should be done under the fundamental guiding principle that what we are after is continually expanding production and consumption of useful goods and services, to be facilitated by larger incomes for consumers and as low prices as can be achieved by large production and the use of efficient methods. In an expanding economy every problem may be solved; in a contracting one all become insoluble.

We come, then, to a recommendation for a large entry of governmental enterprise into fields formerly monopolized by private business—fields in which the product is not free goods or services but rather goods or services sold to the consumer. (This recommendation is not based on any doctrinaire belief in socialism.) Nor is it greatly concerned with the old argument concerning the relative "efficiency" of private versus public operation—such efficiency being customarily judged mainly by the amount of profit made or the managerial practices followed in the individual undertaking. It is based on the fact that government can do a specific job in our national economy that private enterprise has failed to do in important sectors. It can greatly enlarge and continue the investment of new capital. It can reduce prices, improve quality, and so increase consumption. By virtue of both these activities it can aid employment and enhance the national income. By these means it can contribute greatly to the over-all efficiency of our economy, even if we should find—as I do not believe would be the case—that in its individual enterprises there is a somewhat lower standard of productive efficiency than in comparable private establishments.

Management of a publicly owned enterprise need not be any less intelligent or more subject to politics or bureaucracy than management of a privately owned one of the same size and nature. If there were space, examples could be adduced to support this assertion. We have new devices, like the publicly owned corporation, to carry on essential public business. We have the professionalization of administration, checked by modern standards of accounting and performance. But let us grant, for the purposes of argument, that there is an unavoidable inferiority of public enterprise in this respect. There remains an important point often overlooked in discussions of this nature—a point that has to do with the efficiency of the economic system as a whole. Which is more efficient—an economy that employs only three quarters of its workers and of its productive equipment at a high standard of efficiency and has to support the rest in idleness, or an economy that employs all its labor and resources at a somewhat lower standard of efficiency? Un-

less the fully employed economy is very ineffi-
cient indeed, it will yield a larger income and
greater satisfaction than the economy that is
allowing a large part of its productive resources
to go to waste. If private enterprise cannot keep
us busy while public enterprise can do so, we
shall turn more and more to public enterprise.

Government can, by careful advance planning, large-scale operations, and cheap money,
build better houses for a lower price than can
private builders. The bulk of its investment in
good housing is self-liquidating. In housing
projects it acts as a channel for the flow of long-
term credit into new investment—an investment that yields a small but safe return. Such a
procedure does not add to the real burden of
government debt at all. Even if a subsidy is required to make good housing available to
tenants in the lower income classes, the addition
to the national debt which this subsidy entails
is more than balanced by the addition to the
national income which the building operations

provide. There is an almost unlimited opportunity for expansion of activity in rebuilding our cities.

Government could, by taking over the railroads, carry out desirable consolidations, cut the debt burden and amortize what was left, install a rate structure that would increase traffic and employment, and improve the roads by necessary new investment. Even if for a time a bookkeeping deficit resulted, the nation could well afford to pay this deficit out of the general increase in income that would arise from expanded and improved railroad service and railroad orders for materials and equipment.

Government has already demonstrated, in the TVA and elsewhere, its ability to stimulate the use of electric energy and the extension of power lines by a policy of investment and rate reduction. The net result of its activities in this direction, in the fields which it has entered, has been beneficial to employment, the national income, and the standard of living of the consumers. More of the same effort can enlarge its contribution.

To increase the flow of money and to make proper adjustments in the valves of the system through which the flow occurs, it is desirable, then, for the government to enter those types of enterprise where the circumstances of private business have obstructed the necessary expansion of our economy.

It MAY be asked what all this has to do with a constitution. We in America are likely to think of a constitution as a document, based on first principles and worked out in convention by supermen. An economic constitution might therefore be visualized as a sort of utopian scheme for our economic activities, worked out in balanced detail as something completely new and established for all time. But my assumption is rather that a true constitution is a gradual growth, hammered out painfully in the attempt of a society to introduce the kind of order it desires in the face of the conflicting and confused activities of groups and individuals. The process of trying to introduce order into our anarchistic economy is one in which we have long been engaged and with which we are still struggling. It is roughly comparable with the process of welding nation states out of the conflicting principalities and feudal powers that occurred in previous centuries. But the outlines of our new economic constitution are beginning to emerge.

One of its characteristics is increasing intervention by a central government, intervention demanded because our society is in confusion and there is no other agency that can do the job. This intervention is concerned mainly with three kinds of activity—first, providing enough money at the sources; second, seeing that the money is started on its way into use; third, removing obstructions in the circulation of the money through the system. The first activity requires control of banks and credit. This almost everyone accepts, at least in some degree.

The second requires governmental borrowing and spending not merely on relief but also in useful undertakings. This is accepted by a large proportion of the population and will in the end, I believe, be firmly established. The third requires various forms of control over wages and prices, carried out directly in some important instances through governmental enterprise. This kind of activity is rapidly establishing itself.

The common objection to this tendency is that it looks, to the objectors, like a hobgoblin of centralized, dictatorial control over every form of economic function. It might conceivably be that, but as a matter of fact it is not. Like our political constitution, it actually tends to permit greater freedom of some forms of individual and local activity by centralizing those functions which are essential conditions of stability and growth. Extension of government enterprise into monopolistic or basic industries leaves a large area for private initiative, experiment, and competition. The government does not prevent people from making inventions or starting businesses or raising capital for them; its program, if successful, should make new enterprise of this kind more feasible than in the recent past. The government does not interfere with the free choice of consumers; rather it attempts to give them greater purchasing power to exercise that choice and more safeguards against being cheated. It does not restrict recreation or aesthetic activities—but provides better facilities for them. Interference with civil liberties is no part of the program.

Even in the fields where government exercises control, there are many democratic safeguards against dictatorship and more should be created. All are still subject to the inquiry, policy making and checking of our representative political machinery. Extension and improvement of the merit system protects employees against dictatorial political influences. Trade-union organization is a bulwark of economic democracy.

As the new constitution emerges into a more

definite form, it will be essential to accompany it with a planning system, advisory in nature and expert in competence, which will educate us as to the necessities implicit in the situation and so help to safeguard us against the vagaries of executive caprice, the propaganda of pressure groups, or even the mistakes of majorities. In private industry, those establishments that have the least personal autocracy are those that have the best planning staffs. This is because the principles of sound planning are: first, to investigate the facts bearing on the achievement of the objective in view; second, to substitute the authority of the facts for personal authority based on unrealistic or irrational decisions; third, to elicit the coöperation of all concerned in dealing with the problems disclosed.

In this case, as in all others, the question of creating or preserving freedom is as much a question of attitude and response as it is a question of external environment. The times demand better adjustment to environment as a condition of survival. (We are taking environment in this sense to include not merely the physical world but what mankind has made of it, that is, the pressures of society.) The behavior of a society which faces such an adjustment may be compared with the behavior of a child who faces a similar adjustment to the grown-up world. He is born a little anarchist, full of unruly emotions. Somehow these drives must be disciplined and fitted to the conditions under which he has to live. He may reject the adjustment altogether, in which case he is not likely to survive long. Or he may submit without any understanding or coöperation; he becomes dependent on an all-powerful father or mother, whose directions he follows because he fears punishment or loss of their love. This means merely that he has repressed his hostile instincts and remains a child; the primitive aggression is likely to escape in some other form and cause serious trouble for himself and others. In such a situation he is not and cannot be free. But if he is fortunate, he integrates his emotional drives about the problem of adjustment in such a way that the greater part of them can be used. Then he becomes a person capable of self-management, who can dispense with blind obedience to authority because he has learned to recognize external realities, to deal with them, and to coöperate with others in doing so.

Similarly in social life man is again and again confronted by the necessity, for purposes of survival, of developing new disciplines and adjustments. This country at present is subject to a crisis of this kind. We cannot escape the necessity by ignoring it or by living in the dream world of the past. If we merely rebel against the necessity and fail to coördinate our energies intelligently about the task, we shall in the end submit to authority and blindly follow it as it imposes the required discipline upon us. Then we shall lose freedom and democracy. Like the immature person, we shall have to obey orders and self-compulsions in many more details than those genuinely essential for the survival adjustment. The people in a totalitarian state are like children subordinate to an all-powerful and perfect father—the totalitarian leader.

But if we face the facts and deal with them voluntarily and in a constructive spirit, we can become more free and effective than ever before. We can then use central political power as a creative instrument of coöperation rather than making out of it merely a superpoliceman. Here lies the essence of what we mean by democracy. A well-ordered economic constitution is not the enemy of freedom in the modern world but its inevitable accompaniment. In the end it will become clear, if we do a good job in organizing our economic life, that the survival value of democracy is far greater than that of its enemies.

Date Due